∞

*When God Is Silent*

Also available from
Sophia Institute Press
by Luis M. Martinez:

*True Devotion to the Holy Spirit*

Luis M. Martinez

# When God Is Silent

Finding Spiritual Peace
Amid the Storms of Life

SOPHIA INSTITUTE PRESS
Manchester, New Hampshire

*When God Is Silent* was formerly published by Sophia Institute Press in 2000 under the title *When Jesus Sleeps,* an excerpt of three chapters from *Only Jesus* (St. Louis, Missouri: B. Herder Book Company, 1962) with minor editorial revisions to the original text.

*Cover design*: Coronation Media in collaboration
with Perceptions Design Studios.
*On the cover*: "Fisherman" (121909360) © sunipix55 / Shutterstock.com.

Biblical quotations are based on the Catholic Edition of the Revised Standard Version of the Bible, Copyright © 1965, 1966, by the Division of Christian Education of the National Council of the Churches of Christ in the United States of America. Used by permission.

Sophia Institute Press
Box 5284, Manchester, NH 03108
1-800-888-9344
www.SophiaInstitute.com

Sophia Institute Press® is a registered trademark of Sophia Institute.

*Nihil Obstat:* J. S. Considine, O.P., S.T.M., *Censor Deputatus*
*Imprimatur*: Albert Cardinal Meyer, Archbishop of Chicago
May 10, 1962

**Library of Congress Cataloging-in-Publication Data**

Martínez, Luis M. (Luis Maria), 1881-1956.
　　[Only Jesus. Selections]
　　When God is silent : finding spiritual peace amid the storms of life /
Luis M. Martinez.
　　　　pages cm
　　Previously published under title: When Jesus sleeps : finding spiritual
peace amid the storms of life, c2000.
　　Includes bibliographical references and index.
　　ISBN 978-1-62282-220-1 (pbk. : alk. paper)　1. Jesus Christ — Devotional literature.　I. Title.
　　BT306.43.M28 2014
　　232.9 — dc23

2014019299

# Contents

Editor's note: Except where noted otherwise, the biblical references in the following pages are based on the Revised Standard Version of the Old and New Testaments. Where applicable, quotations based on other translations have been cross-referenced with the differing enumeration in the Revised Standard Version, using the following symbol: (RSV =).

∞

*When God Is Silent*

*Chapter One*

# *Rely on Christ when He seems distant*

∞

Through the intuitions of love, more than through the liveliness of the imagination, we have often constructed interiorly an arresting scene: the ominous sky, the wild winds, a little boat tossed by the seething waves of Lake Tiberias, with Jesus asleep in the stern.[1] What a contrast between the fury of the tempest and the sweet, majestic peace of the divine slumber! The omnipotent, the Most High, He who is infinite activity because He is infinite perfection and unfailing felicity, surrendered to that sure sign of limitation and misery: sleep.

What would the sleeping Jesus be like? St. Thérèse of the Child Jesus[2] states that children please their

[1] Matt. 8:23-27; Mark 4:36-41; Luke 8:22-25.

[2] St. Thérèse of Lisieux (1873-1897), Carmelite nun.

5

parents just as well asleep as awake. To souls enamored of Jesus, the Beloved is as beautiful in the silence of His sleep as in the zenith of His activity. Jesus is always beautiful, always great, always divine, "altogether desirable,"[3] as the Song of Solomon declares.

The gentle Virgin Mary often contemplated the ineffable beauty of Jesus asleep. With the eyes of a mother, a lover, and an artist, she enjoyed the celestial delight of that marvelous divine beauty. What mildness in that incomparably comely countenance! What harmony in that motionless body! What majesty in that sweet repose! What radiations emanated from that sacred humanity quietly resting there.

Jesus was exceedingly beautiful when He spoke words of eternal life, accomplished wonders, looked with love, pardoned with mercy, and caressed with tenderness. But I would like to have seen Him while He was sleeping because I could have contemplated

[3] Song of Sol. 5:16.

Him to my heart's content, without the fascination of His gaze distracting me, without the perfection of His beauty and the glory of His splendor dazzling my eyes and enrapturing my soul. The beauty of Jesus awake is too great for my smallness. Who could support it? I feel it more suited to me veiled by sleep, as the glory of the sun is more adapted to my eyes when I look at it through a translucent lens.

Mary most holy must have watched the sleep of Jesus many times. Mary's ecstatic eyes would never tire of looking at her divine Son. With holy liberty, she covered Him with the kisses of her virginal lips as her immaculate hands caressed Him tenderly. If we had seen Jesus asleep, small and helpless as we are, we too would have dared to caress Him without reserve and to lull His mystical sleep with our timorous but ardent kisses.

Great artists striving to express the contrasts involved in the strength of repose have succeeded in producing the impression of an immobility filled with power, a calm of restrained activity, an activity that is its own mistress. Through the magic of art, incompatibles — majestic repose and animated activity — are united.

Through a divine art, this mighty contrast is realized in an indescribable manner in Jesus asleep. With the person of Jesus, the phrase of the Song of Solomon, "I slept, but my heart was awake,"[4] is not a figure of speech used in the language of love, but a profound reality of the divine order. His sleep was like ours, because He took on Himself our miseries. His exterior and interior senses during sleep had that mysterious ligature which wise men have not yet explained satisfactorily. Sleep was not for Him, as it is for us, a suspension of our active life mingled with an occasional flash or mysterious phantasm of light and action. Although the lower part of His most holy soul was plunged in shadows, the higher part opened fully to

[4] Song of Sol. 5:2.

the light of glory and the Beatific Vision far beyond the need of bodily aid, nourished in the unfailing torrent of the divinity.

The profound understanding of Jesus was flooded with celestial splendor. Beatific love burned in His Heart, enveloping with flames of blessedness and glory that Sacred Heart ever alert for love, ever living to make to His Father the holocaust of His tenderness, ever active to pour into souls the treasures of His mercy.

In the presence of that regal immobility and the divine silence of that most comely body, could one guess the interior glory? Through the delicate, celestial veil of human sleep, could penetrating and loving eyes like those of the Virgin discover the deep secret of the interior joy of Jesus?

The Apostles, with their narrow, human judgment, because they had not yet received from the Paraclete the deep sense of the divine, did not suspect on Tiberias the mystery of that Heart which was always watching.

Frightened by the din of the storm, they awakened Jesus to command the winds and the tempest. "Why are you afraid? Have you no faith?"[5] the Master asked them. They did not yet have it in the plenitude they were to receive in the Cenacle.[6] They did not understand that even though we need to be awake to exercise our limited activity, Jesus, even as man, concealed under the mystery of His sleep the limitless power of the Beatific Vision.

Who can comprehend the sleep of Jesus? Who can conceive the strikingly beautiful contrast between the summit of that soul bathed in the light of glory and the lower part covered with the shadows of sleep, like the earth immersed in the sun's glory in one hemisphere and submerged in the calm of night in the other?

---

[5] Mark 4:40.

[6] The upper room in which the Last Supper took place and where the Apostles received the Holy Spirit on Pentecost.

Rely on Christ when He seems distant

∞

*Christ works in your soul even as He sleeps*

Jesus lives mystically in souls, reproducing in them all the mysteries of His mortal life. With the keen intuition of her love, St. Thérèse of the Child Jesus understood the mystery of this mystical sleep, expressing it with her inimitable language, full of ingenuous and truest poetry: "Jesus slept in my boat, as was His wont. But how rarely will souls allow Him to sleep in peace. Wearied with making continual advances, our good Master readily avails Himself of the repose I offer Him, and in all probability will sleep on till my great and everlasting retreat; this, however, rather rejoices than grieves me."[7]

Who else would have thought of interpreting the dark, painful chasm of spiritual desolation with such amiable, heavenly light? Almost all souls are disconcerted by desolation. They conclude that Jesus has

[7] *Saint Thérèse of Lisieux, the Little Flower of Jesus* (New York: P. J. Kenedy and Sons, 1927), 134.

11

gone away, that the sweet visits of former times, bright
and fragrant as a spring garden, were a fleeting dream,
an idyl interrupted through their own infidelity and
ingratitude. They fear that the love so sweet, so deep,
and so sure, to which Jesus invited them, has been
turned into hate, as happens to all love that meets
with neglect. In their unspeakable agony, these poor
souls hold the firm conviction that the Beloved has
fled from them, perhaps not to return, bearing away
with Him the entrancing perfumes of Heaven, the
divine clarity that illuminated life's pathway, and
the holy consolations superior to all earthly joys.

These desolate souls surmise everything except
that Jesus is only sleeping within them, just as He
slept in the little bark on Tiberias while the wind
roared and the tempest raged. Only the pure eyes
of the gentle child of Lisieux, only her gaze of love
could discover the secret of a lover. Jesus has not gone
away, nor will He ever leave, because love, strong as
death, never departs, and its divine ardor cannot be

extinguished by the torrents of our ingratitude. Jesus continues to live in the soul to whom He pledged love, because His name is *Faithful and True*.[8] He sleeps sweetly in that soul which belongs to Him, because it surrendered itself to Him, attracted by His irresistible fragrance.

Could that consoling idea of St. Thérèse of the Child Jesus be an effort of an ingenuous and charming optimism to cover with a veil of piety the blackness of a terrible pain in order to endure it, or is there hidden under a precious symbolism a profound reality concealed from the eyes of the wise and prudent and revealed only to the little ones?[9] The exceedingly deep love of the Carmelite virgin for truth and her remarkable sanctity, attested to by the Church, shows unmistakably that the girl saw clearly and deeply into the divine mystery. Jesus needs to sleep in souls so that

[8] Rev. 19:11.
[9] Cf. Matt. 11:25.

they may contemplate the exquisite beauty of His slumber, so that the divine Heart which watches while He sleeps may accomplish in silence the prodigies of purity and love that Jesus ordinarily accomplishes only in the midst of tempests and in the mystery of His sleep.

∞

Like the Apostles, souls want to awaken Jesus when the storm threatens. What will they do without Him? Passions that seem conquered rise with new vigor. A darkness like that of death covers the sky of the soul, once a bright blue. The whistling of a hurricane disturbs the soul with gloomy, desolate, despairing ideas that seem to come out of Hell. The frail little bark of the soul is about to capsize, and Jesus sleeps. "Master," the soul cries to Him, like the Apostles on Lake Tiberias, "do You not care if we perish?"[10] And Jesus, when He does awake — the time of trial seems

[10]Cf. Mark 4:38.

so prolonged — speaks to the soul as to the disciples in the little boat: "Why are you afraid? Have you no faith?"

Just as it was unnecessary to awaken Jesus on Tiberias, it is unnecessary that He be awake in souls to give them life. The words of the Song of Solomon may also be applied to His mystical sleep: "I sleep, but my heart watches." Yes, Jesus watches solicitously in souls that love, even though they feel that He has abandoned them. Love does not abandon. Jesus is there in the depth of the soul. He seems to sleep because the soul does not hear His refreshing voice, because it does not enjoy His celestial consolations. But the Heart of Jesus is always watching with His inextinguishable love, with His incessant actions, with His tender care more solicitous each day.

If only one might know the fecundity of Jesus in His mystical sleep! He works in the soul with the same efficacy as when awake — perhaps with greater efficacy. Divine consolations dilate the heart, calm the passions, and quiet the soul, filling it with the mildest unction. Desolations also accomplish the work of God — a delicate, profound work of purity, strength, and love. There are certain delicate and intimate operations that Jesus does not perform in souls except when He is sleeping. His mystical sleep is not from weariness, but from love. He sleeps because He loves. He sleeps because, while He sleeps, His Heart watches, transforming souls profoundly, although this transformation is imperceptible.

St. Thérèse of the Child Jesus saw secrets of the spiritual life with remarkable clarity, and in order to explain why she was not grieved by her aridity in prayer and her naps during her thanksgivings, she observed that doctors put their patients to sleep in order to perform operations. It is likewise necessary for Jesus to place souls under a holy sedative, into complete darkness, into absolute unconsciousness, to accomplish in them divine operations. When this occurs, the soul thinks Jesus is sleeping.

## Rely on Christ when He seems distant

How would souls be able to endure those awful sufferings which, like double-edged swords, penetrate even to the depths of their being, if Jesus were awake, if that sweetest of voices resounded in them, if the fragrance of His life penetrated their spirit, if they experienced the divine action clearly and palpably? With Jesus manifest, one does not suffer. Looking at Him and receiving His caresses, the soul becomes a replica of Paradise. When He shows Himself, sufferings are either dissipated like vapor before the heat of the sun, or are turned into a brilliant and beautiful vision. The soul needs to suffer in its innermost being, and to suffer for a long time, and to suffer without much consolation. In order that the soul may suffer in this way and thus receive special graces, Jesus sleeps.

*Let faith and love sustain you while Jesus sleeps*

The grace of purifying and fruitful sorrow is assured by the sleep of Jesus in the soul. As the tempest on

17

## When God Is Silent

Tiberias coincided with the sleep of the Master, so in souls the hurricane rages when Jesus sleeps. Souls need to be tempered in the clamor of the storm. They must be shaken by the seething waves to learn the stability of love. The sky must be overcast so that in the midst of shadows they may catch sight of the mysterious light of faith. The very depths must be opened beneath their fragile bark, so they may know how to hope against all hope.

The ancients believed that pearls were formed when the ocean was shaken by a storm. The precious pearl of divine love (the possession of which causes one to despise all earthly things) is formed within the spotless shell of the soul precisely at the dreadful but fecund hour of desolation.

Together with the grace of suffering, spiritual tempests bring the grace of humility, a new, deep humility that hollows out in the soul a void so immense that God fits into it. When Jesus is awake and shows Himself to the soul in all His celestial beauty, when His divine lips speak of love and life, and when His infinite action becomes a delight, the soul has neither eyes nor time nor desire to look at itself adorned with the precious jewels from its Beloved. But when He sleeps, the night that envelops the soul with its cold, sorrowful darkness, obliges the soul to gaze upon itself in astonishment, to experience its wretchedness, to feel its powerlessness, and to be lost in the abyss of its nothingness. From the depths of that abyss, humility arises by divine magic, and the soul, even if elevated to the third heaven, will never forget the repulsive sight of its own misery which it contemplated, horror-stricken, in the sad night while Jesus slept and the tempest roared.

Incredible as it may seem, it is necessary that Jesus sleep in order to refine love and purify the soul. At first sight, we might believe there is nothing better than divine consolation to inflame souls with love. Was it not consolation that made the soul turn its eyes toward Jesus in the first place? Was it not He, attractive, resplendent, loving, who passed near the soul like a vision of life and happiness, saying to it as to the Apostles, "Come, follow me,"[11] making the soul leave everything to run after Him "to the sweet smell of His ointments"?[12] So, let not that vision of Heaven be fleeting. Let Jesus always show Himself to the soul. Let Him speak words of love to it. Let Him charm it with His radiant beauty. Let Him establish His dwelling within it. Upon the summit of radiant Tabor, the soul's love will be converted into fire, into passion, into Heaven.

But this is not the way that love is purified. Love, purest gold from Heaven, mixed with earthly dross, needs the fire of suffering to recover the limpidity and brilliance proper to its celestial origin. When Jesus is awake, He gives more than He receives. The soul can scarcely do anything else than receive the

[11]Matt. 19:21.

[12]Cf. Cant. 4:10 (Douay-Rheims translation; RSV = Song of Sol. 4:10).

divine infusions. When night comes, when Jesus surrenders to sleep, He moves the soul to correspond to the love it has received, to give generously, to offer its bitter tears and its secret martyrdom with heroic fortitude.

This precious prerogative of love did not escape St. Thérèse of Lisieux. Nothing escapes the intuitions of love! "And now, dear Mother, what can I tell you about my thanksgivings after Communion, not only then but always? There is no time when I have less consolation — yet this is not to be wondered at, since it is not for my own satisfaction that I desire to receive our Lord, but solely to give Him pleasure."[13]

Most souls in their recourse to God seek in Him their own satisfaction. They go after consolations and sweetness. They think about themselves, about giving themselves pleasure, and not about pleasing their Beloved. They have true love, but it is imperfect. Blessed

[13]*Saint Thérèse of Lisieux, the Little Flower of Jesus*, 142.

are the souls who, like St. Thérèse of the Child Jesus, await God's visit only to please Him. Blessed are the souls who know how to watch over the slumbers of Jesus and peacefully await His radiant awakening. Blessed are those who shower upon Him loving caresses while He sleeps, converting their tears into pearls of pure love and their bitterness into sweet consolation. The love that forgets itself to think about the Beloved, that suffers so that He may rejoice, that watches so He may sleep, that weeps in secret so He may rest in silence and peace, is love pure and undefiled, born only of suffering and desolation, despoiled of the gross dross of egoism.

∞

Oh, if one could understand the value of desolation! If one could appreciate the austere but exquisite beauty of Jesus when He is sleeping! But suffering souls neither suspect the mystery they guard in their hearts, nor do they have the serenity to contemplate the extraordinary beauty of Him who sleeps within them, just as the Apostles, worried by the storm and overcome by fear, did not enjoy the divine spectacle of Jesus asleep in the storm.

When Jesus sleeps in a soul, the enraptured angels must contemplate that mystery of fruitfulness and beauty, for desolation has its beauty just as the deep, arid ravines have their beauty, as do the sheer, gigantic cliffs, bare of verdure, to which only the soaring eagle has access.

But how to appreciate that beauty in the night of the soul, among the shadows guarding the sleep of Jesus? There is a subtle, penetrating light shining in the darkness. It is the light of faith. When it is living, when it is nourished by love, when it receives from the Holy Spirit an unknown divine penetration and mighty power, it manifests to souls who allow Jesus to sleep, who watch His sleep, and who suffer so He may rest the hidden and mysterious spectacle of Jesus sleeping — a most beautiful contrast of silence, dark-ness, and sadness.

∽

O souls enamored of Jesus, offer Him your pure and loving hearts so that He may come to rest therein. Permit Him to sleep as much as He wants while you, silent and tender, watch His mystical slumber. Fear neither the silence nor the darkness that guard the mystery of that sleep. Do not awake the sweet Beloved, because His Heart is watching when He sleeps, and the apparent inaction of that repose hides prodigies of productivity that will transform your life.

Be quiet in the midst of your grief, so He may not awaken. Weep in silence, so that your tears may be pearls of love for Him. Cover Him with your tender caresses, with your timid but ardent kisses. Open your eyes, "the illuminated eyes of your heart," to contemplate the hidden beauty of Jesus asleep. One day — a day of rejoicing, of light, of rapture — Jesus will awake, and upon seeing that you have offered Him the warm, silent, perfumed couch of your heart, and that you have watched tenderly and solicitously during this slumber of love, He will command the winds and the tempest so that the peace of Heaven may reign in you, and in the depth of that most sweet peace, the mystery of love will be realized, happy, and never-ending.

*Chapter Two*

∞

# *Listen for God in*
# *peaceful silence*

∞

One of the most admirable characteristics found in the life of Jesus Christ, our Master and our Model, is silence. All the mysteries of His mortal life and the ineffable mystery of His eucharistic life have this mark: the divine seal of silence.

Holy Church tells us that Jesus came to this world in the midst of universal silence: "While gentle silence enveloped all things, and night in its swift course was now half gone, Thy all-powerful Word leaped from Heaven, from the royal throne."[14] The first thirty years of the life of Jesus were wrapped in an impressive silence. Afterward came the three years of His public life. This was the time for speaking, the time for communicating

[14]Wisd. 18:14-15.

with men. Yet even this period contains marvels of silence. Silence is something so characteristic of Christ's Passion that the prophet commented on it, saying, "Like a lamb that is led to the slaughter, and like a sheep that before its shearers is dumb, so He opened not His mouth."[15]

In His eucharistic life, does not that unfathomable silence enveloping the Eucharist impress us profoundly and communicate itself to us when we approach?

Silence is not classified as a virtue, but it is the atmosphere in which virtues develop. At the same time, it is a sign of their maturity. Thus, just as we know that when the golden spikes of wheat appear in the field, the grain is ripe, so also, when a virtue is tinted with silence, we perceive that it is reaching maturity.

Let us make some reflections upon the silence of Jesus and try to reproduce it in our heart so that we can imitate it in our lives.

[15]Isa. 53:7.

# Listen for God in peaceful silence

∞

*Learn to practice interior silence*

Let us consider the silence of Jesus during His hidden life, that is, the first thirty years of His life. This silence is truly inexplicable. If there had ever been a man with the right to speak, with all the gifts for attracting attention, with all the means to create a stir, that man was Jesus, because He was the Eternal Word of the Father, uncreated Wisdom, the Master whom men had awaited for so many centuries. Certainly, if there is any single event in history that merits a stir in its behalf, it is the coming of Christ to live among us. But instead, a hush shrouds His first thirty years.

The Gospel, speaking to us of these years, is restrained, almost mute. Many times we would like to know a little more of the mysteries of the infancy of Jesus to nourish our piety. But the Gospel makes only an occasional reference to the episodes of His first years. A few pages refer to the hidden life of our Lord, and each incident mentioned, like murmurs heard in quiet fields, emphasizes and accentuates the silence rather than destroys it: the adoration of the Magi,[16] the flight into Egypt,[17] the going up to the Temple[18] — three events that do not disturb the silence of the hidden life, but make it more evident.

We feel this silence in a special manner in the house of Nazareth. It is the "house of silence"; we cannot conceive of it in any other way. Its very mention enshrines our souls in silence. When we meditate on the mysteries enacted there, we feel that all who dwelled there were divinely silent.

St. Joseph: not a single word of his has been preserved for us in the Gospel, and we cannot imagine him except as enraptured in silent contemplation of those mysteries taking place around him.

The most holy Virgin was silent too, with that silence of wonder and of love which the presence of

[16]Matt. 2:1-2, 11.
[17]Matt. 2:13-14.
[18]Luke 2:41-50.

Jesus produced in her; a silence augmented by His holy illumination and by the mysteries that she witnessed and in which she participated. The Gospel presents one mysterious statement that allows us to catch a glimmering view, as it were, of the abyss of silence and contemplation in the heart of the most holy Virgin. Having narrated those mysteries, the Gospel adds: "His mother kept all these things in her heart."[19] She did not discuss them with St. Joseph, but she preserved them and meditated upon them within her own soul.

And Jesus, especially working in St. Joseph's shop, must have led a silent life with His soul and heart absorbed in the heavenly Father, His soul and His Heart united in prevision to ours, dreaming dreams of love and of pain, thinking about the glory He would give to His Father and the good He would do for souls. His spirit was absorbed in the mysteries of the kingdom of

[19]Luke 2:51.

33

## When God Is Silent

Heaven. As I see it, this silence is the silence of contemplation, the silence of the interior life.

∞

Silence, even naturally speaking, invites us to concentrate within ourselves and to think about serious, profound things. For example, when we are in the forest, upon the ocean, or in the desert, we experience the necessity of concentrating, of recollecting ourselves. Such is our psychological structure that noise forces us outside of ourselves, distracting us and scattering our powers; it forces our spirit to go skipping around through external things. But when silence prevails, we concentrate again; once more we live within.

In accordance with this law of our psychology, we need to live within in order to live with God, because we always find God in the interior of our soul. It is natural that exterior silence is not only an invitation to an interior life, but also a necessary condition for that life of intimate communication with God. The atmosphere of the interior life, of the contemplative life, is silence; hence, the masters of the spiritual life recommend it so highly. Therefore, it is one of the most fundamental observances of the religious life.

In order to live the contemplative life, in order to live the religious life in any of its forms, and even for all true interior life, exterior silence is indispensable. To realize its importance in living above and not below, in living a life of intimacy and union with God, let us not lose sight of the fact that silence should not be treated as a mere disciplinary measure or as a means of order such as is found in a school or in a class, but as a necessary condition for living within and not living without.

At first glance, one may think that speech is superior to silence and that we communicate with God by speaking and singing, because song, as someone has said, is the language of love. Is not Heaven the eternal abode of contemplation and of love? And in Heaven, one sings without ceasing. Isaiah and St. John listened to the new canticle of glory: "Holy, holy, holy is the Lord God of hosts,"[20] which the blessed never cease singing day or night. Well, now, is not the Christian life the prelude and the beginning of the life of glory? Why, then, is silence necessary upon earth in order to communicate with God?

The silence of which I speak, of which Jesus gave us the example in Nazareth, is not the absolute lack of words and spiritual canticles. Assuredly, Jesus must have lived during the thirty years of His hidden life in an intimate and uninterrupted conversation with His heavenly Father. When His lips were silent, His Heart spoke in a manner more eloquent, more divine. Exterior silence is not silence with God but with creatures.

The contemplative life is an intimate affair; it is a loving conversation of man with God. But in order that God may speak to the soul and the soul speak with God, it is necessary that there be silence. Neither

[20]Cf. Isa. 6:3; Rev. 4:8.

God nor our heart will be silent, but the earth and created things must be hushed, because everything worldly hinders the intimate conversation of our soul with God.

This silence is not the silence of the desert nor of the tomb — a negative silence, the lack or suspension of life. It is like the apparel of a more interior life that one wears outside, because inside he is singing a love song. He does not speak with creatures, because he is speaking with God; he does not listen to the noise of earth, so that he may hear the harmonies of Heaven.

As an audience maintains silence to hear better the voice of an orator, as music lovers keep silence during a symphony to admire its artistic beauty, so the silence of contemplation is nothing other than the indispensable condition for hearing the voice of God and addressing to Him our heartfelt words.

∞

Silence is not only the indispensable condition for the development of the interior life, but it is also, as I said at the beginning, a sign of the maturity of virtue. When the interior life reaches a certain degree of development, it is marked by silence. In the beginning, we have some difficulty in speaking with God, but as our intimacy with God increases, our conversation with Him becomes easier, because His love provokes an inexhaustible source of loving words in our innermost soul. If this love continues growing until it reaches a certain degree, if our friendship with Jesus becomes more intimate and perfect, then words begin to fail us, because they seem impotent to express the sentiments of our heart. Little by little, words disappear, and our communication with God becomes the divine communication of silence.

Even in conversations among men, we find these different stages. When one person begins to communicate with another, if either or both lack confidence, conversation is difficult. Afterward, when both have become friends, the difficulty disappears, and the conversation can be prolonged for hours. But if this friendship develops into a deep affection, a moment will come in which words do not suffice. Then speech gives way to silence. The great emotions of the heart, like profound sentiments of the soul, are not expressed with words but with silence.

Silence has two functions in the contemplative life. At the beginning and at all times, it provides the environment for developing the spirit of contemplation. Silence quiets all creatures so that God may speak. It cuts the communication with outside affairs and puts us in intimate contact with God. It concentrates all our energy on our interior and makes our life a living prayer. Afterward, when contemplation has reached a notable degree of maturity, silence is not only its guardian but also its supreme expression and most intimate language.

How does one practice this silence of contemplation? I have nothing to say of exterior silence, because its rules are well known. On the other hand, when exterior silence is not kept, ordinarily it is because there is no silence in the interior of the heart. Without doubt, exterior silence helps the interior, but exterior silence is not kept perfectly when it is not observed within. Therefore, let us speak of interior silence.

If we want to attain silence in the interior of our hearts, we ought to begin by investigating the causes of the clamor within us. Ordinarily there are two causes of interior noise: the imagination and the heart.

How often it happens that we enter the presence of Jesus to converse sweetly with Him, and then the imagination begins to skip around, carrying us hither and thither. Sometimes it is nothing definite that attracts us, but simply the incessant mobility of that faculty of ours. We want to find it, but it flits around like a butterfly, stopping here and there, tracing improbable curves in the interior of our soul. Thence comes the noise; it is the imagination that disturbs interior silence.

At other times, the source of the din is in the heart. Except in cases of abnormal agitation, the imagination never produces the clamor that the heart produces. When we are under the stress of some particular emotion, such as love, fear, desire, or anger, we cannot compose our spirit; our soul seems like a city full of noise. One single passion often produces a greater clatter in the soul than that which jars our nerves in an industrial city. When a disturbance arises from the imagination, it is transitory; but when the heart is the source, how difficult it is to be recollected, and how tense is our whole soul!

When we suffer, pain produces a constant and monotonous noise; a single word is spoken to us, but it is a word that disturbs our entire being. On the other hand, when we love intensely, that same word repeated to us completely satisfies our heart, but it rules out every other voice.

Consequently, in order that silence may reign in our heart, it is necessary that the heart and the imagination be hushed, or at least that they make a sound suited to what we want to hear. That is what happens on a liturgical feast: the religious music, the liturgical hymns, and the chiming of bells raise us to God, because there is harmony between what we hear exteriorly and what we hear interiorly. That same thing can happen in our soul, when our heart and our imagination are making the same sound that we must make to Jesus.

To quiet the imagination is difficult, but it is necessary to moderate it. It is not necessary to treat it with violence, nor to subject it by force, nor to chain it up. When the imagination is subjected to force, it becomes even more aroused. Such a procedure is comparable to chaining a dog and beating him to make him stop barking; instead of becoming silent, he will bark more and his bark will become more intolerable. Tact is necessary to manage the imagination. When this faculty is aroused, it is wiser to direct its activity into channels that more closely correspond to our purpose, rather than to strive to quiet it.

If, for physiological or psychological reasons, I have an excited imagination and I want to approach Jesus to converse with Him, what shall I do? Take the imagination and enclose it in a prison? That is impossible. What shall I do, then?

The same that one would do with a broken record. If we cannot make it play properly, we change the record. In place of worldly songs, we shall introduce religious music that supports our purpose. This is the way to deal with the imagination; it is useless to attempt to shackle it, because it will not be shackled. Let us "change the record," replacing it with one that is in harmony with God.

The heart is silent when all its affections are concentrated on the love of God; it is silent when there are no discordant, scattered notes, when all its tones rise toward Him.

The silence that we are discussing is the silence of the earthly and the human in order that the divine may resound in us. It is evident that as the heart empties itself of discordant sentiments and of affections out of harmony with the cry of the love of God, silence becomes orientated in our soul.

For interior silence, one needs detachment. If we consider the matter well, the only thing that cries out within us is love. When the love of God possesses us completely, we bear within our heart a close resemblance to the eternal Trisagion,[21] and in our exile we begin the prelude of the new canticle of the Fatherland. But when there are other affections that are not those of Jesus, there is a cacophony that hinders us in our contemplation and our love. In order to keep interior silence, therefore, we must chain our passions and rid the heart of earthly affections.

There is another remedy. Have you not had the experience of being in church at some religious function, and when the organ stopped playing and the liturgical hymns ceased, you heard the cries of vendors, the murmurs of passersby and various other street sounds? But

[21]"Holy God, Holy and Mighty One, Holy and Immortal One, have mercy on us."

suddenly, the organ resumed its powerful overtones, voices again intoned the sacred canticles, and you no longer heard what was outside because the harmony within was too intense. Thus, there is another way of establishing silence in our heart: by making contemplation and love more intense than the external distractions. The silence that is asked of us is a relative silence; it is the calming of exterior noise so that the new canticle of our love may resound with increased harmony and intensity.

To manage our imagination prudently, to divest our heart of all emotion that hampers the love of God, and to make contemplation and love more ardent in our souls, I give you here some efficacious means, expressed in a general way, for waging an effective campaign against interior noise and for creating silence in the depth of our souls. Little by little, we shall imitate the silence of the hidden life, and our heart will be a replica of that sweetest of mysteries, the ineffable silence of Nazareth.

∞

*Let prudence and charity govern your silence*

At first sight, it seems that Jesus broke His divine silence during the three years of His public life. It would not be strange; in fact, Scripture affirms that there is a time to speak and a time to keep silence.[22] But I think that if our Lord interrupted that profound silence of contemplation which characterized His life in Nazareth, He did not fail to practice in an admirable manner — or it well may be in a still more admirable way — the virtue of silence during the agitated years of His apostolic life.

How much time during those three years our Lord dedicated expressly to contemplation! Some passages in the Gospel give us to understand that Jesus used to go at night to some solitary place, frequently to the top of a mountain or hill, and there He would pass the night absorbed in silence and love.

[22]Eccles. 3:7.

Yet it is not precisely to our Lord's silence of contemplation in the midst of His public life that I wish to refer to now. But I do think that in the midst of His apostolic ministry, our Lord practiced silence in a less obvious manner than He had done in Nazareth, but very difficult for us and in reality very perfect. I refer to the silence of discretion and of charity — not an absolute silence, but a relative silence; a silence that we also ought to practice constantly in our relations with our neighbor.

We know that many times Jesus must have desired to express what was in His Heart, but He remained silent. Prudence, discretion, and charity sealed His lips so that He practiced a costly silence.

How many things Jesus would pass over in silence! For example, when He spoke of the Eucharist in Capernaum,[23] if He had followed the impulses of His Heart, how much He would have said, since the Eucharist

[23]John 6:25 ff.

was the ideal, the dream that He had cherished during His whole life because it satisfied all the desires of His love here upon earth. But discretion indicated to Him what He ought to say and what He ought to leave unsaid. We know that in such cases it is more difficult to know how to keep silent than it is to speak.

Our Lord must have experienced often the necessity of reprimanding the multitudes and even the Apostles themselves in order to restrain abuses and vulgarities that offended His most refined soul. Nevertheless, charity required that He remain silent.

I maintain that one of the greatest griefs that afflicted our Lord during His public life — if we except the interior sorrows that tormented Him during His entire life — was to have to deal with all those poor souls who were so far from Him. Even for us simple mortals, how distressing it is to have to deal with persons of a different mentality, different education, or contrary temperament. Let us imagine what it would be like to live constantly with men of misguided ideas, with infidels, or with persons of complete moral degradation. Without going to these extremes, how often it is a true torment to deal with those who are more like ourselves but on whose account we must make constant sacrifices in order to live with them.

With greater reason was this true in the case of the sensitive soul of Jesus. Therefore, I believe that because of their crass ignorance, torpidity of spirit, and coarseness of feelings, the persons who surrounded Jesus must have been thorns piercing His Divine Heart.

Of all the souls with whom Jesus had to deal, the Apostles were the best and most select; yet how slow they were to understand His teachings, how imprudent in speaking when they should have remained silent. On one occasion, our Lord, attacking the scrupulous and exaggerated practices of the Pharisees, had just explained to the multitudes that to eat without washing the hands does not defile a man: "Not what goes into the mouth defiles a man, but what comes out of the mouth, this defiles a man."[24] And although the explanation was very clear, the Apostles did not understand, and they made our Lord explain still further. He did so, but one understands that He suffered on account of their limited intelligence.

Although it is true that, on some occasions, our Lord was obliged to reprove His Apostles in view of their spiritual formation — now for the slowness of their minds in understanding His teachings, again for the crude ambition that led them to dispute about the first places, at another time for the imprudence of their impulsive characters — nevertheless our Lord maintained silence on many another provocative occasion.

This silence of discretion and of charity is much more costly than the silence of contemplation. Doubtless it sometimes demands effort to keep contemplative silence, but ordinarily this is not the case. Silence

[24]Matt. 15:11.

in the midst of words, silence in communicating with our neighbor is much more distressing. A thousand times we would like to exteriorize that which we carry within, and thus unburden ourselves. On a great many other occasions, we have to conquer ourselves, enveloping ourselves in a silence of prudence and charity.

On the other hand, the Heart of Jesus was as human as ours, and consequently it must have experienced the urge to unburden griefs just as we do, especially when His Heart was harboring deep secrets, immense griefs, and great sorrows. Nevertheless, to have to repress the disclosure of His troubles, to have to hide His most intimate feelings, and to have to speak like the others as if He carried in His soul only what is lowly and ordinary — is not this an arduous and difficult silence?

It is also a perfect silence; that is to say, it presupposes a certain degree of perfection in virtue. The apostle St. James says that the one who knows how to restrain his tongue is a perfect man.[25] Therefore, knowing how to restrain the tongue is a sign of perfection and sanctity. To possess the judgment and the discretion necessary to speak when one ought to speak and to keep silence when one ought to be silent requires such an assemblage of virtues that the one who attains it is a perfect soul.

When the enemies of Jesus sent their spies to listen deceitfully to His preaching and to apprehend Him, they became frightened and did not touch Him. When asked why they had not carried out their orders, they answered, "No man ever spoke like this man!"[26] And we might add, "No man ever knew how to keep silence like this man." No one, in truth, has known how to keep the silence of prudence and charity as Jesus has, and he who arrives at practicing all that charity and prudence demand in regard to silence is a perfect man.

[25] James 3:2.
[26] John 7:46.

## Listen for God in peaceful silence

The practice of this silence demands in a special manner the practice of two virtues: prudence and charity. Prudence is one of the most difficult virtues to acquire. When we consider all that one must remember, foresee, and think of in order to act with prudence, we can understand that without the special assistance of grace, it would be exceedingly difficult to practice this virtue.

On the other hand, it is not seldom that, when we are most desirous of speaking, when we feel most eager to express ourselves, this is the time that prudence directs us to be silent. And if we do not heed this inspiration, we ourselves can verify the consequences of a single imprudent word. How many times we have repented of a fleeting word spoken without reflection! On the contrary, how many falls one avoids, how many anxieties one escapes, if he knows how to practice the surpassing science of silence. To know how to keep timely silence is the perfect work of prudence.

In order to govern our tongue, charity is united to prudence. The same apostle, St. James, teaches us that it is easier to steer a ship or to master an unruly colt than to manage our tongue, in spite of its being so small an organ.[27] Therefore, to succeed, prudence and charity must join hands.

Doubtless, charity makes us speak many times, now to defend our neighbor unjustly defamed, again to make his good qualities evident, at another time to counsel him in his doubts and to console him in his griefs. But perhaps there are more occasions on which charity obliges us to maintain silence, for charity demands that we avoid every word, however insignificant, that may wound our neighbor. Charity is so exquisite, our neighbor is so sensitive, and so earnest is the desire of our Lord that we preserve this virtue unblemished, that we must constantly watch our tongue so that it never utters a word that would

[27]James 3:3-5.

offend our neighbor and injure the sacred rights of charity.

How beautiful is the silence of charity! Our Lord gave us an outstanding example of this when, after His Resurrection, appearing to His Apostles singly or in groups, He did not reproach them in the least for having deserted Him in so cowardly a fashion. He did not utter a word to Peter himself about his denial, contenting Himself with asking for a triple confession of his love.[28] Is not this silence of Jesus touching and admirable? Any one of us would have given in to the impulse of manifesting his feeling in some manner. We would at least have said to Peter in an injured tone, "Why did you abandon me in the hour of trial? You especially, Peter, who in the Cenacle declared that you were ready to die with me, why did you deny your Master? Nevertheless, I pardon you. Peace be with you!" Our Lord did not say this. Rather, it seems that His love and the

[28] John 21:15-17.

sweetness of His words go to extremes: "Peace be with you. . . . Fear not. . . . It is I."

Oh, if we might imitate Jesus in this silence!

If we really love our neighbor as Jesus loves us and as He asks us to love, we shall keep silent about our neighbor's defects and even about that which might embarrass him, although it is not properly a defect. We shall avoid all disclosures that may pain him, even when it satisfies our wounded self-love. We shall not set about investigating whether this word wounds him much or little, because the charity that is disposed to avoid only serious offenses is a very immature charity; rather, we ought to avoid all that can even remotely offend him. Paraphrasing St. Paul, who said that if the fact that he ate a certain food would scandalize his neighbor, he would never eat it,[29] we ought to say, "If this word offends my neighbor, I will never say it."

[29] 1 Cor. 8:13.

# Listen for God in peaceful silence

∞

*Learn when to bear your sufferings silently*

In His most sacred Passion, Jesus gave us an admirable example of a new form of silence: silence in pain. Sometimes it is exceedingly painful to keep silence; sometimes silence increases and revives the bitterness of grief. Our Lord gives us an example of these two forms of painful silence in His Passion.

We see an illustration of the first when Jesus, appearing before the tribunal of the Roman proconsul Pilate, was acquainted with all that was charged against Him. "Do You not hear," Pilate questioned, "how many things they testify against You?" And the Evangelist adds, "But He gave them no answer, not even to a single charge; so that the governor wondered greatly."[30]

How irritating this silence must have been for Jesus to keep! When false testimonies were given and calumnies uttered against Him, He must have

[30]Matt. 27:13-14.

experienced a burning impulse to speak — not so
much to avoid death, since He had already accepted it
generously and determinedly for the love of His Father
for our souls, but for the sake of justice, for His honor,
and for the justification of His holy conduct. With but
one word, Jesus would have been able to discredit the
accusations and justify Himself, yet He kept silent. Is
not this silence of Jesus heroic?

Many times we find ourselves in a situation that
calls for imitation of Jesus in this silence. To keep still
when, with one word, we could manifest our innocence
and cancel out all charges against us is frustrating, is
heroic, but how often it is necessary. To be quiet then,
to choose not to excuse ourselves when we could,
through love of humility, is a silence that imitates
Jesus in His Passion.

If we analyze the Gospel attentively, we find that
sometimes Jesus defended Himself and sometimes
He preferred to remain silent. For example, in the
presence of Annas, when one of the guards gave

Him a blow, Jesus justified Himself: "If I have spoken wrongly, bear witness to the wrong; but if I have spoken rightly, why do you strike me?"[31] But before Pilate, as we saw, Jesus kept silence.

Our Lord's course of action on these occasions is nothing more than an application of the maxim in Scripture: "A time to keep silence and a time to speak."[32] In a general way, it can be said that when it is for the honor of God or the good of our neighbor, we ought to speak. When it concerns only ourselves, it is almost always more perfect to keep silence, in imitation of our Lord in His Passion.

In the Passion of our Lord, there is still another more heroic silence, the one Isaiah foretold when he said that Jesus would be carried as a sheep to the slaughter, without uttering a sound.[33]

[31] John 18:23.
[32] Eccles. 3:7.
[33] Isa. 53:7.

## When God Is Silent

In order to understand this silence, one must ponder the immense grief Christ bore within His soul. Every possible torture had been heaped upon His body, every ignominy poured into His soul. He was one incurable bleeding wound, as the prophets had foretold.[34] His enemies did not spare Him one single humiliation, from parading Him in disgrace through the streets of Jerusalem to nailing Him, naked, on the infamous gibbet of the Cross, between two thieves and amid the blasphemies of His foes. His sacred honor was mocked with a crowd's sneer.

In His Heart He carried the "terror of the grave,"[35] far beyond our comprehension, but which some few souls have been privileged to perceive indistinctly as in a darkened glass.

If any one of us should have to suffer, not what Jesus suffered, for that is impossible, but even an

[34] Isa. 1:6.
[35] Ps. 17:6 (Knox translation; RSV = Ps. 18:5).

exceedingly small part thereof, it would suffice to make us scream and grit our teeth with pain. And Jesus was silent — like a sheep led to the slaughter, without a murmur, in a wondrous silence!

Only twice Jesus seems to have manifested His grief: once in Gethsemane, when He complained to His Apostles because they could not watch even one hour with Him,[36] and again, on Calvary, when He allowed to escape from His dying lips that poignant complaint: "My God, my God, why hast Thou forsaken me?"[37] But those two outpourings from His Heart do not come as interruptions of His heroic silence, because their purpose was to teach us two important lessons, rather than to mitigate His grief.

In the first place, He wished to show us that sometimes we can and ought to unburden our heart. He knew very well that there would be in our lives

[36]Cf. Matt. 26:40; Mark 14:37.
[37]Matt. 27:46.

especially sorrowful moments in which, because of our weakness, we would experience the need of crying out. So that we might not be ashamed to do so at that time, He wanted to manifest the heaviness of His Heart by crying out, not for His comfort, but for our consolation.

In the second place, He wanted to give us a fleeting vision of the profound sorrows of His Heart. If He had not complained, we would not have found any testimony of them in the Gospel.

There are souls to whom God has given as a special vocation to know, venerate, and love the interior cross of the Heart of Christ, that is to say, His innermost griefs — what might be called the "passion of the heart and the heart of the Passion."[38] These souls needed a revelation, the testimony of the Gospel concerning those sorrows which, like a flash of lightning, reveal a little of the sorrowful mystery of the Heart of Christ.

[38] Msgr. Charles Gay, *Entretiens sur les mystères du Rosaire*.

With the exception of these two disclosures, Jesus was silent during His Passion.

Let us admire that silence kept in sorrow and try to imitate it. Alas, how many times sorrow indiscreetly manifested to others dissipates its fragrance and loses all its perfume. For sorrow resembles those delicate perfumes that evaporate quickly and therefore need to be kept in hermetically sealed urns. Grief is an exquisite perfume, precious in the eyes of God. For this reason, we ought to guard it with the greatest care in the vase of our heart, so that its fragrance will not dissipate.

Without doubt, it is most painful to keep the vase of our suffering closed. To share our suffering with others alleviates our heart's cruel pain, but it diminishes the value of suffering. Silence in sorrow — that is to say, suffering without lament — gives to our grief its highest value and rarest perfume.

This does not mean that we should never manifest our sufferings. Jesus Himself manifested His on two occasions — in Gethsemane and on Calvary — to teach us that we, too, in certain circumstances and with discretion, should reveal ours. Sometimes we need to express ourselves, because if we did not, sorrow would suffocate us. Weak, limited in capacity for suffering as for everything else, we must allow a little of grief's perfume to escape, so that we may have the capacity to suffer more, so that suffering may not overwhelm us with its oppressive weight. Sometimes we need to disclose our griefs for just and holy purposes, such as asking for light, direction, or a rule of conduct to be followed.

But with the exception of those cases, the perfection of sorrow lies in silence.

Did we not say that silence is for many virtues the sign of maturity? When love is very intense, it expresses itself in silence; when sorrow has attained its perfection, it shares in the triumphant silence with which Jesus endured the inexpressible pangs of His Passion and death.

# Listen for God in peaceful silence

∞

*Christ communicates His love*
*through the silence of the Eucharist*

But I have yet to speak of another august silence of Jesus: the silence of love, the silence of the Eucharist. Few things impress us so much in this incomparable sacrament as the silence that has enveloped it for twenty centuries. The quiet of the tabernacle impresses us even physically when we approach it and, with greater reason, when we concentrate on the mystery of the Eucharist, contemplating therein the silent Christ.

The very state in which Jesus is found in the Most Holy Sacrament is a state of silence. According to theologians, He cannot speak, nor can He make use of His senses without a miracle. St. Alphonsus Liguori[39] says that He is deprived in such a way of the use of His senses and is so impotent for all things else that it

[39] St. Alphonsus Liguori (1696-1787), moral theologian and founder of the Redemptorists.

65

seems that here He has only one free activity: the activity of the heart; that He placed Himself in that state so that He might have nothing else to do but to love.

And so it is in very truth. Jesus in the Sacred Host does not speak; He knows only how to love. In an evil hour, His enemies come and profane the Sacrament of His love, but Jesus is silent. Sacrilegiously they open their stained lips to receive Him, but Jesus is silent. He does not take a whip as in the Temple of Jerusalem to punish the profaners. He does not throw into their teeth their sacrilege as He did the hypocrisy of the Pharisees. Jesus is silent, and for twenty centuries that sacred, unfathomable silence has endured. Simply because He loves, love has bound His lips and His hands. Love has reduced Him to silence.

But is not that silence the most eloquent proof of His immense love? Oh, assuredly we feel the love of Jesus when we listen to Him on the eve of His Passion, speaking to us the profound words of the discourse at the Last Supper. But perhaps we feel it more in the Sacrament of His love, hushed and silent. We do not lament that Jesus does not speak to us from the Sacred Host; His silence is more eloquent and expressive.

Sometimes we, who do not understand sublime and lofty things, complain, saying, "What a pity that Jesus does not speak from the tabernacle; it would be so sweet to listen to His words!" I think that it is better that He does not speak, because with His silence He expresses perhaps better than with His words the love that He professes for us.

Let us not forget it: the summit of love is silence. Love that can still be expressed with words has not arrived at its perfection, nor reached its culmination. Our words are too restricted, too feeble, to express what is great and limitless. Have we not realized that the deepest impressions of our souls cannot be expressed with words? When grief reaches its climax, it becomes silent. When the friends of Job who had gone to visit him saw him oppressed by every evil and in a state of terrible pain, the Scripture states that they remained in silence for seven days and seven nights because their grief was too great to be expressed with words.[40]

And thus it always happens to us: when we see a splendid spectacle of nature, we are silent. Ordinary sights, on the contrary, make us talk, and we gayly comment on them. Something sublime imposes silence. Therefore, admiration, sorrow, love, all the great sentiments of our heart, and all the deep impressions of our soul are like this: when imperfect and limited, they can be expressed with human speech; when they increase and reach their peak, they cannot be expressed by weak words. Their only language is silence.

In Heaven, love is not expressed in this way because another language — not of this earth — exists there. Here below, the greatest love is silent love. Such is the love of Jesus in the Eucharist. Happy are we if we love Jesus with that sublime silence! Many a

[40]Job 2:13.

time our love speaks, our love sings, our love expresses itself in diverse manners. But when love increases in our heart, it tends to become silent. The fact is that then it has reached maturity; it has become so intense, so deep, that it cannot be expressed with our dull human language.

Let us understand the silence of the Eucharist and put ourselves in unison with Jesus in that wondrous stillness. Every day we can enjoy that most sweet silence. Have we not experienced in our heart the deepest impression of the eucharistic silence? Have we not felt our souls enfolded, as it were, in that silence of love?

That silence teaches us more than words, and it tells us how much Jesus loves us. It is also contagious, for, having possessed our hearts, it soothes us, calms us, and moves us to express our feelings, with the same incomparable language of silence.

I do not mean by this that we always approach God in silence. No! Love takes many forms and has many manifestations. Let us leave our heart at liberty to speak, to sing, to be quiet. Especially, let us allow ourselves to be guided by the Holy Spirit, where He wills and as He wills. But what I am attempting to say is that there exists a sublime silence of love, that there is a way of communicating with Jesus in silence.

St. Thérèse of the Child Jesus used to say that our Lord is a master who teaches without words. In fact, His silence is doctrine, instruction, and eloquence; His silence seems to penetrate even to the core of our souls, teaching us great truths.

When we approach the tabernacle, let us not try to hear the words of Jesus. Rather let us listen to His silence. Let us permit that silence to envelop and penetrate us even to our innermost being, and it will teach us more than all the words that we desire to hear.

∽

*Silence will prepare you for Heaven*

From this rapid review of the different forms of Jesus' silence — the silence of contemplation, the silence of prudence, the silence of pain, and the silence of love — how many lessons we can draw forth to our soul's advantage! We have already noted some of them. Jesus spent the first thirty years of His life wrapped in contemplative silence. His public life was spent in the silence of charity and prudence. His Passion was bound up in a sorrowful silence, and He lives the eucharistic life in a silence of love. We ought to copy all these types of silence in our lives and reproduce them in our hearts.

We should live in an atmosphere of silence so that the divine flower of contemplation may flourish therein. In dealing with our neighbor, we must exercise many times, like Jesus, the silence of prudence and charity. And, as victims, we ought to offer ourselves, in union with Jesus, to the heavenly Father for souls.

Thus, in the midst of these holy forms of silence, our life will pass, preparing us for the true, eternal life where we shall intone a new canticle, a heavenly canticle. But it seems to me that, even in Heaven, that canticle would be expressed in silence. Why? Because in Heaven all is silent except God; all is silent; only the word of love resounds. Doubtless, here on earth, we hear the voice of God, and we pronounce the word of love, but the din of creatures disturbs us, and many times we must interrupt our song. Not so in Heaven. There all is hushed; no noise of creatures breaks the grand silence. There is but one note, one word, the one that comes forth from the Heart of God and from our own hearts: the word of love.

But do not the blessed in Heaven hear the clamor that rises from the earth? Certainly, but in Heaven those words have another meaning. St. Paul says that on the final day of time, Jesus will triumph over all His enemies and the last of God's enemies to be destroyed will be death. Once His enemies have been defeated, our Lord will take all men and subject them to God in order that "God may be all in all."[41]

---

[41] 1 Cor. 15:28 (Douay-Rheims translation).

## Listen for God in peaceful silence

Inscrutable expression! What does it mean that God may be all in all things? We do not now comprehend the profound meaning of creation, or of history, or of the universe. We hear the noises of the earth in a superficial manner, and therefore they disturb us. But then, "God will be all in all," and all the sounds that reach even to the skies will speak to us only of God.

Therefore, we can well say that there is not, nor will there ever be, a silence similar to the silence of eternity, to the silence of Heaven, because there every creature is silent and there is heard only one sound — God; only one word — the word of love.

*Chapter Three*

*Follow the three
paths to peace*

∾

When the angels announced to the world the incomparable, unprecedented joy of Jesus' birth, they made two promises: one in favor of Heaven, the other in favor of earth; the former, the *glory of God,* the latter, *peace to men of good will.* Both of these pledges include and summarize the entire work of Jesus Christ in this world: to give glory to God and to bring peace to souls.

As it would not be possible to discuss within the compass of some few pages these two sublime objectives of Jesus' work, I shall confine my considerations to but one of them: peace.

Peace is the gift that Jesus Christ brought us from Heaven — His gift, the gift of God; a gift so beautiful, so profound, so all-embracing, so efficacious that we shall never truly comprehend it.

When God Is Silent

We might say concerning peace what our Lord said of Himself to the Samaritan woman at Jacob's well: "If you knew the gift of God . . ."[42] Truly, if we but understood this God-given gift of peace, we could appreciate how it is the synthesis, the very climax, so to speak, of all the graces and heavenly blessings that we have received in Christ Jesus.

Peace is the seal of Christ. It is not just one of His many gifts; it is, in a certain way, His own gift. When Jesus appeared in the world on that unforgettable night in Bethlehem, the angels proclaimed peace. On another unforgettable night, the last that He spent on earth, the sweet night of the Cenacle and the Eucharist, Jesus left peace to His loved ones as a testament of His love: "Peace I leave with you; my peace I give to you."[43]

Our Lord's customary greeting to His Apostles after His Resurrection was this: "Peace be with you."[44]

[42]John 4:10.
[43]John 14:27.
[44]Cf. John 20:21, 26.

## Follow the three paths to peace

Furthermore, He recommended that, in pursuing their apostolic mission, they should always say these words upon arriving at any house: "Peace be to this house," and if a son of peace dwelled there, he would receive their peace; if not, their good wishes for peace would redound to themselves.[45]

Holy Church, the perpetuation of Jesus throughout the centuries, understands our Lord's spirit thoroughly. Adopting her Master's expression in her Liturgy, she constantly invokes peace upon her children. While imparting peace to us, she disposes us to give peace to one another. Almost all the sacramental rites terminate with an expression of peace. The newly baptized, the Christian strengthened by Confirmation, the sinner purified in the sacrament of Penance — all receive a message of peace: "Peace be with you" or "Go in peace."

The communication of our Lord's peace sometimes takes place in an external ceremony, full of tenderness.

[45]Luke 10:5-6.

When God Is Silent

It may be an embrace, as in a Mass, between the celebrant and the assisting ministers; it may be a kiss of peace, as between the bishop and the priest he has just ordained. The entire Liturgy is impregnated with this spirit of Christ; at every turn, it echoes Jesus' word to His Apostles after the Resurrection: "Peace be with you."

The life of the Church is nothing else than the triumphant march of peace throughout the world. Above the cradle of the Church, as above the manger of Bethlehem, angels could fittingly sing the same canticle: "Glory to God in the highest, and on earth peace to men of good will,"[46] for the Church has done nothing else, nor does she intend to do anything else, than to give glory to God and peace to men of good will. She has no other mission.

Our Lord's peace has distinctive characteristics that call for at least a brief consideration. First, it is a

[46]Luke 2:14 (Douay-Rheims translation).

peace *exclusively His own;* He has a monopoly on peace. On the eve of His Passion, He said to His disciples: "My peace I give to you; not as the world gives do I give to you."[47]

The world, which counterfeits everything, cannot counterfeit peace, however much it tries. It misrepresents joy; the world's happiness is always superficial and sometimes even bitter. The world counterfeits wisdom, dazzling the credulous with a showy but empty knowledge. It counterfeits love, giving this sacred name to brute passion or to vile egoism. The world, the offspring of Satan, father of lies,[48] is essentially an impostor, falsifying everything. But it is powerless in counterfeiting one thing: peace. The world cannot give peace, because peace is a divine thing; it is the seal of Jesus Christ.

A second characteristic of our Lord's peace is its *profundity.* It is not superficial, merely exterior, the

[47]John 14:27.
[48]John 8:44.

peace of the tomb or the desert. Such is not really peace, but solitude, emptiness, desolation. The peace of God, on the other hand, reaches even to the depths of our hearts. It pervades our innermost being, penetrating it like an exquisite perfume. Peace is plenitude; it is life.

Third, peace is *indestructible*. Nothing, no one, can force the peace of Heaven out of a soul that has received this gift of God; neither the persecutions of tyrants, nor the snares of the Devil, nor the vicissitudes of earth can disturb a soul in which God has established His peace.

On the eve of His Passion, Jesus, having told His Apostles that He gave them His joy, added, "Your hearts will rejoice, and no one will take your joy from you."[49] Precisely the same may be said of peace: "And no one take it away from you." Everything else may be taken away from us — our homes, our property, our

[49]John 16:22.

liberty, and even our life. In a certain sense, we can be deprived of happiness. It is true that perfect joy can be experienced precisely when the eyes weep and the heart bleeds, but such heights are characteristic of only very elevated, perfect souls. Consequently, enemies may take from us, in some measure, even our joy. But they can never deprive us of peace when Jesus has given it to us. Peace can continue its reign in our hearts in spite of the miseries, sadness, and bitterness of life.

Finally, the peace of Christ is a *rich* peace, full of sweetness and mildness. St. Paul describes it as "the peace of God, which surpasses all understanding."[50] This peace is the only form of happiness unparalleled upon the earth; it is the substance of Heaven. Without the splendors of the Beatific Vision, without the overflowing happiness of that everlasting state, peace is the substance of what we hope to enjoy in Heaven.

---

[50]Phil. 4:7 (Douay-Rheims translation).

## When God Is Silent

∞

Nineteen centuries have passed since Jesus made this richest of gifts to humanity. Each Christmas He renews this heavenly gift in souls and the angels again sing, "Peace on earth to men of good will." Each Easter Jesus, risen again, greets the faithful with His favorite expression: "Peace be with you," pouring into Christian hearts a veritable torrent of peace.

I am not referring at the moment to exterior, collective, or international peace. On the contrary, I refer to interior peace, which wars and persecutions cannot disturb. Why, I insist, is peace so greatly lacking in souls? I understand that there are struggles and sufferings within the soul; but what seems difficult to comprehend, if one thinks deeply, is that peace should be lacking in the soul of a Christian.

We Christians have a claim on suffering, struggle, and persecution, but we have no claim to the loss of our peace. The proper attitude and natural atmosphere of the Christian should be one of peace, and in the midst of all the vicissitudes of life, he ought to preserve peace, the seal of Jesus and the characteristic feature of the Christian.

Where God is, there is peace, and we carry God in our hearts. Neither life nor death, neither the powers of Heaven nor the forces of Hell, neither height nor depth, nor any created thing whatsoever can draw out of our heart that God whom we possess.[51] Then why is not our whole life utterly filled with peace?

I am emphasizing this point because I maintain that souls ought to preserve peace at all costs. In order to do this, it is essential to discover the secret of peace.

Holy Scripture says, "Seek peace, and pursue it,"[52] thus pointing out to us that peace is not to be sought with lukewarmness and negligence, but with ardor, with care. In war, one pursues the enemy; in peace,

[51]Cf. Rom. 8:38-39.
[52]Ps. 34:14.

one seeks happiness. In the same way, we ought constantly to seek and pursue peace.

But is it always possible to preserve peace of soul? Should our hearts never be disturbed by anything at all? Are there safe, direct routes to reach this most blessed goal?

Undoubtedly there are. But the strange thing is that souls lose peace so easily and then live in turmoil. This is a real evil. But what of suffering, struggle, and desolation? Let them come! But anxiety, disturbance — never! Sufferings conceal sweet, celestial fruit under their bitter rind; anxiety and disturbance never contain any good.

Our Lord never asks, nor can He ask, the sacrifice of peace even of souls entrusted with a mission of suffering. He will ask them for the sacrifice of all earthly goods. He will ask them for the painful, life-long immolation of themselves. He will ask them for interior, tormenting holocausts, but always in an atmosphere of peace.

It would be interesting to make an analysis of our anxieties, but we would be ashamed of the ignorance, the egoism, and the distrust causing them. Rather than analyze the evil, I prefer to set forth the means whereby the soul may preserve peace despite all obstacles.

∞

*Faith in God's love and Providence brings peace*

The first path to peace is faith. In fact, if we lived by faith, we would live in peace. We read in Scripture, "My righteous one shall live by faith."[53] He who lives under the rule of Faith lives in perfect peace; all Faith's teachings tend to calm us.

Let us make a synthesis of the teachings of Faith relative to the subject we are treating, to help us realize the facility with which we may attain peace when we live supernaturally. Faith teaches that God loves us

[53]Heb. 10:38.

and that He loves us not as a group, but personally, individually: "He loved *me!*"[54] Each one of us can make these words of the apostle Paul his own without fear of error. He knows my name; He has engraved my image in His Heart. Still more, I can be assured that His Heart is all mine, because our Lord cannot love as we do, by halves; when He loves, He loves with His whole Heart, infinitely.

Souls sometimes say, with a mixture of love and of ignorance, "I wish our Lord would love me more." But is that possible? Can He who loves infinitely love any more? If nothing else existed in the world except God and you, O soul who reads these lines, He would not love you more than He does right now. If you were the only object of His love, He would love you just as He loves you now.

God's love has all the characteristics of the love we idealize in our ardent dreams, for we all dream; it so

[54] Cf. Gal. 2:20.

becomes the human heart to dream. Yes, we want to be loved with a deep, tender, consuming love. Half measures do not satisfy us, nor do they satisfy elect souls destined for intimate union with God, those souls tortured by the insatiable desires of love.

Now, let me assure you of this: Jesus loves us more, infinitely more, than we desire, more than we dare to dream of. Sometimes our dreams seem bold, almost absurd; nevertheless, they are far below reality.

It is this very magnitude of God's love that so frequently disconcerts us. We think, "It is an exaggeration to say God loves me like that. If not even I can love myself that way, how is it possible that God does so? No, that is an excess."

Right, it is an excess; infinite love has to be so. The Incarnation, the manger, Nazareth, the Cenacle, Gethsemane, Calvary — each was an excess. And the Church and Pentecost are other tremendous excesses, because they are the works of an infinite love. In comparison with our smallness, infinite love must necessarily be an excess. Yet, how difficult to convince souls that God so loves them. If they could be convinced, how many anxieties would be alleviated.

∞

We may go a step farther. God's love for us is not a sterile love, confined to Heaven. It is an active love, provident, watchful, and solicitous. It is a love that does not forget us for one moment, that protects us unceasingly, that keeps arranging minutely all the events of our life from the most far-reaching to the most insignificant.

I am not exaggerating; Jesus Himself affirmed it: "Not a hair of your head will perish."[55] Some persons may consider this hyperbole. Perhaps, but, at any rate, it is a hyperbole expressive of the solicitude, the constancy, and the minute care of God's love for us.

Consider a mother caring for her first baby, watching at his cradle, ever mindful of his needs, anxious

[55]Luke 21:18.

lest he cry or become ill. The devotion of such a mother cannot match even remotely the constant, minute, tender solicitude of our Lord.

If only we had the faith to understand this. Not for one moment does our Lord turn His eyes away from us, nor does His hand cease to guide us; at each instant of our lives, His power protects us and His love enfolds us.

And if this is true, if God's solicitude for us is loving, unalterable, and most tender, what reason have we to be disturbed? Can a child in his mother's arms be disturbed? Only in one way: only if he dreams that he is in danger and alone. His uneasiness would be the fruit of an illusion. If the child realizes that he is in the arms of the mother who loves and protects him, why should he be restless? Through what strange phenomenon, through what inexplicable illusion do we Christians disquiet ourselves, knowing with the certainty of faith that a loving God bears us in His arms and surrounds us with His divine tenderness?

# When God Is Silent

Let us penetrate this mystery of love and of mercy a little farther. Let us see what are the sources of our own most frequent anxieties. Frequently, we become disturbed by thoughts like these: "Could I have committed that fault?" "Shall I get rid of these temptations?" "Am I in a good state before God?" "Am I on the right road?" "Will my superiors change my place or my work?" "Have I lost the trust and esteem of my superiors?" If I am ill: "Shall I get well?" If I am well: "Shall I become ill?" If I tried to make a complete list of all our worries, I would never finish; each reader may complete it on his own.

Ordinarily, we concern ourselves about future events as well as those that are past. Well now, did all these disquieting events escape God's loving Providence? Or could our Lord have been distracted when He determined that such a thing happen to us? Or was He unable to avert this event in spite of His attention and solicitude for us? Or did His love suffer an eclipse during which this misfortune befell us?

By no means. What does happen is that we forget that God arranges or permits all things, that nothing escapes His Providence, and that our Lord guides and governs our whole life. When we are disquieted, it is usually through such forgetfulness or because the event is not according to our liking and we do not accept it with resignation, or because we want to know the consequences beforehand, whether for good or for ill. "Will this affair involve me in complications? Will it not be the first link in a chain of sufferings and contradictions?"

We forget that God regulates all things, that we are not alone, but carried in the divine arms, those omnipotent arms, which not only protect us, but also direct the world and arrange all of life's occurrences. Since we are in such hands, protected by such love, are we not foolish to be disturbed?

∞

The peace enjoyed by the saints intrigues us at times, but we wonder how they always remained tranquil in the midst of so many painful vicissitudes. To me, it seems still stranger that Christians, who have the Faith, are filled with anxiety, for to preserve peace, one single thing would suffice: to live by faith, especially to believe in the consoling dogma of the love of God and of His constant, solicitous Providence. We should need nothing more.

"What will tomorrow bring? What will happen to me this year? Will it be better or worse than last year?" Idle questions, useless forebodings. I know only one thing: that today as yesterday, that tomorrow as today, that this year as last, God loves me, and He loves me as my heart yearns to be loved — no, much more than I dare aspire to. I know only that during this year as in the past I shall continue to live in the arms and in the Heart of Jesus, and that He, with incomparable solicitude, will rule over all things, including each detail of my life, designing all for my good and for my happiness.

Since this is true, no one need wish me happiness in the new year; I carry happiness in my heart. If I become ill, if I am persecuted, if I am dying — these are incidents of no importance. In reality, all these things will contribute to strengthen my peace and to increase my happiness. In utmost tranquillity, therefore, I rest in the arms and in the Heart of Jesus. My heart echoes Bethlehem's hymn: "Glory to God in the highest, and on earth peace to men of good will." My soul resounds with the tender accents of Jesus' farewell: "My peace I leave you."

Let us recall an anecdote about Julius Caesar. He was crossing a river in a boat. Suddenly, the winds were unleashed, and rough waves rose high. The boatsman hesitated, trembling. Julius Caesar haughtily rebuked him, saying, "Why do you fear? You are carrying Caesar." As if Caesar had the power to chain the winds and to soothe the waves! But the story reminds us of another phrase more wonderful still: "Why do you fear? You are carried by Jesus!" Jesus guides you; Jesus takes you in His arms; Jesus bears you in His Heart.

## When God Is Silent

A living faith, especially faith in the sweet, consoling dogma of our Lord's love for us, is one of the most direct and sure ways to achieve peace. If God loves me, if He cares for me constantly, if His Heart's loving solicitude attends every event of my life, I can and I ought to live in peace.

But it may be objected: Do the love of God and His Providence really influence all the events of our lives? Perhaps our liberty — that God-given gift at once glorious and terrible — may snatch our affairs and our destiny out of His hands, so to speak, and place upon them the seal of turmoil, changing them into means of affliction.

We readily agree that some of life's situations are arranged by God — that we are here or there, healthy or ill, in desolation or in consolation — but it is difficult to regard others in the same way. For example, persecution against the Church — is this also providential? Is this not out of harmony with the love of God?

And there is something still more difficult to reconcile with God's loving Providence — namely, our failings, our sins. How is it possible to commit faults and go astray if we are in God's arms? Can a person sin within the Heart of God? Why does our Lord permit falls, especially a certain kind of fall? We pass over some faults easily, because they are slight or less humiliating or of little importance, but there are others that disconcert us, that seem to change our life. "Lord, how did You permit such a thing? Could that moment of my life possibly have eluded Your attention?"

St. Paul gives us a very concise, enlightening principle in this respect: "Everything helps to secure the good of those who love God."[56] Let us take that *everything* just as it sounds, without exceptions, including certain temptations and circumstances seemingly unfavorable for our sanctification, our defects, and especially our falls. We must make no exception where God

---

[56]Rom. 8:28 (Knox translation).

makes none. *Everything* helps to secure our good —
consequently, this includes persecutions from without
and struggles from within, dangers and temptations,
our defects, and our very falls. All things work together
for the good of those who love God.

I am among those who love God; therefore, I abso-
lutely should not be disturbed by anything that may
happen to me. If I become ill, blessed be God; this in-
firmity will sanctify me. If I am well, blessed be God;
health will be a means of doing good. If persecution
oppresses me, blessed be God; it will jolt me out of my
lukewarmness. If persecution ceases, blessed be God; I
can now devote myself to my sanctification with
greater liberty. If I am tempted, if I fall into sin, how
good, O Lord, that Thou hast humbled me, so that I
may learn to know and despise myself.

Let no one think that I am trying to give a lesson in
artificial optimism, emphasizing the fair side of everything in order to ward off suffering. Much less am I
proposing a system of ease. May God deliver me, when

speaking in His name, from advancing a human system, however perfect and ingenious. No, I speak only the truth in Christ Jesus, and I do nothing more than explain the doctrine contained in the Scriptures: "Everything helps to secure the good of those who love God."

From this, it follows that the knowledge of events in store for me is a very secondary matter, because I already know that whatever their nature, they will bring me to God. A traveler whose chief concern is to arrive safe at a certain distant country regards the mode of travel as of secondary importance. He reaches one station of the trip and asks, "How does one travel here?" "By train." And he takes the train. "And here?" "By automobile." "And here?" "By plane." "And here?" "By boat." It is a question of greater or less comfort, of greater or less speed, but for the one who seeks neither comfort nor speed, but who is intent only upon reaching the end of his journey, the means is a very secondary matter.

## When God Is Silent

What does the journey matter, provided one reaches sanctity? The main thing is to reach it. What does it matter whether we go to God through sickness or through health, through struggle or repose, through consolation or aridity? If we ourselves set about selecting the way, in all probability we would choose sweetness and ease — and the wrong route — whereas our Lord chooses for us what we need at any given moment. The worst thing that could happen to us would be to be given freedom of choice in selecting our own path to Heaven, for our selection would be unwise; we would choose desolation when in need of consolation, and consolation when desolation would be more suitable; we would choose struggle when rest would be in order, and rest when effort would be necessary. We would never make the right selection, because we are too shortsighted to know ourselves, the designs of God, or the paths to perfection. St. Paul says that we do not even know what we should ask for — so simple a thing — and therefore the Holy Spirit asks for us:

"The Spirit helps us in our weakness; for we do not know how to pray as we ought, but the Spirit Himself intercedes for us."[57]

A keen realization of this truth should convince us that the best thing for us at each step is what God sends. Frequently, it is not to our taste, but what does it matter, provided we are sanctified? What means are at hand today for my sanctification? Whatever God sends me — whether it be sickness, temptation, or aridity.

The fact is that we would like, in greater or lesser degree, to please ourselves; or rather, to please ourselves in a merely natural order rather than in a supernatural order. So we often would like one thing or another for our own comfort, through self-love; and if what God sends us is not to our taste, we are disturbed and even rebellious. In the spiritual order, too, we would like to satisfy our personal tastes. I want to reach sanctity, but

[57]Rom. 8:26.

by this path, in imitation of my favorite saint. But no, our Lord knows better than we along what path and in what manner we must reach Heaven.

On the other hand, we would like to have clear insight into all that happens to us and its contribution to our sanctification. And so when we understand that such a thing will sanctify us, we are content; but if we do not understand, we are disquieted. How can this suffering possibly sanctify me? The Cross is indeed the way to perfection, but there are crosses and there are crosses, and in this one I see no prospect of coming closer to God. How shall I become holy if our Lord places me in these conditions that seem opposed to my sanctification?

What blindness of heart! Do you not understand the ways of God? He loves you more than you love yourself. He loves you more than anyone else loves you. He is unceasingly solicitous for your good. If He sends you this cross, it is exactly what you need for your sanctification.

## Follow the three paths to peace

If we but understood these truths, what could make us lose peace? How calm our lives would be! Come this event or another, it makes no difference — in the depths of the soul, I mean, for, not being of stone, I shall not fail to feel. Some events bring joy and others, suffering; yes, I shall suffer and weep and I may even complain, but deep in my heart I shall experience peace. *Lord, this instrument You are now using to sanctify me must be very precious since Your love sends it. Yes, I recognize it but it pains me. Allow me, then, to weep and to complain.* And Jesus allows us to weep and to complain, but what He does not want is that we become disturbed; while we groan and weep, He would have us preserve peace in our heart.

Things seen superficially can disturb us, but if we regard them with the profundity of faith, nothing can make us lose peace. One day St. Ignatius Loyola[58] was asked if anything could alter his peace. The saint

[58]St. Ignatius Loyola (c. 1491-1556), founder of the Society of Jesus, also known as the Jesuits.

replied, "Only one thing could disturb me, the sup-
pression of the Society; but I believe that a few moments would suffice to calm that disturbance and to
recover peace."

Then no difficulty exists; all things work together
unto good for those who love God, for, in the divine
hands, even hindrances are converted into helps.

∞

But does moral evil, sin, also promote the spiritual
welfare of those who love God? Yes, the apostle excepts
nothing, and neither should we: *all*, even our failings,
even our sins. But is it possible that sins work toward
the good of those who love God? Some simple reflections will suffice to clarify this point.

The sacrifice of Jesus was the greatest event in human history, the most fruitful, the most efficacious, or
to speak more accurately, it was the only efficacious
sacrifice, since it is the source of all efficacy in the supernatural order. Did not the sacrifice of Jesus require
as an instrument the greatest sins ever committed on

earth? Does not Holy Church describe the very sin of Adam as "happy" because it gave occasion for Christ to come to redeem us? On Holy Saturday, the Church sings, "O happy fault that merited such and so great a Redeemer! O truly necessary sin of Adam!" What audacity in the Church to speak thus! But it is the audacity of profound insight.

Since the time of Adam's Fall, God has this invariable strategy both in the general history of the human race and in the history of each soul: to draw good out of evil, which thereby becomes an instrument to achieve good. History proves this perfectly. The cowardice of Pilate, the cunning of Caiphas, and the intriguing, haughty spirit of the priestly leaders and the scribes and Pharisees were the ladder along which Jesus went to His sacrifice. The tyranny of the Caesars during the first three centuries of the Church gave rise to the multitude of glorious martyrs. The heretics, who continued the persecutions, gave occasion to that group of Fathers and Doctors of the Church. Thus, in the succession of events, God always draws good out of evil.

What God does on a large scale in history, He does on a small scale in each soul. One day in Heaven, we shall understand the important role played in our sanctification by our frailties and our sins. And even though we regret having offended God, after all, perhaps we should paraphrase the words of the Church: "O happy sins of mine that merited so great a Redeemer." O truly necessary faults, for our failings humiliate us by revealing to us our nothingness. This is one of the main purposes for which God permits them.

But let us be sincere. Are our faults repugnant to us, and do they grieve us only and exclusively because they are offenses against God? Do not motives of shame frequently prevail, such as the blemish of these faults, the wound to self-love, and the like? Similarly, we want to be freed from temptations not only to be less exposed to the danger of offending God, but also to avoid the annoyance of a struggle against them.

This being so, is it not true that it would be a very simple, efficacious, and gentle procedure to let ourselves be sanctified by accepting each day what our Lord asks of us? We have absolute certainty that what God plans for us each day is most suitable and sanctifying.

Sometimes in the morning we are too far-seeing; we would like to take in from the first moment the whole course of the day: "What shall I have to do? What am I going to suffer? What do I fear? What do I hope for?" And we set up our program.

The only program for me is God's program. Let this day come as it may; God sends it — He and no one else. Let it come as it may; we are sure that it comes wrapped in the love of our Lord and destined to sanctify us. We ought to say, "I will be sanctified precisely by the events of this day, because the loving Providence of God has sent them to me. He is acquainted with my necessities. He knows what is most conducive to my sanctification." If we were to understand this, would not our soul be a veritable ocean of peace?

∞

One final objection: I acknowledge that by following God's plan and subjecting myself to His will, I walk in security and live in peace. But anxieties arise on this account, for, by the abuse of my liberty, I may resist the divine will, go astray, and follow a crooked path. Is not this a reasonable cause for worry? No. It is a reasonable cause for repentance, for tears and a firm resolution, but not for the loss of peace. God does not cease being good because I am bad, nor does He cease seeking me because I go astray. Did He not reveal to us His own Heart in the parable of the good shepherd who left the ninety-nine sheep while he ran after the one that was lost?[59] Yes, I have absolute certainty that if I go astray, Jesus will seek me. I shall place myself in His omnipotent hands. I shall rest upon His shoulders,

[59]Matt. 18:12; Luke 15:4.

and I shall return to the fold. Perhaps I must suffer to return to the right path, but blessed be the sufferings that atone for my fault and bring me back to my God.

Whatever our failings may be, whatever our wanderings, we have no right to lose either hope or peace. We are Christians, and we Christians have received peace as a gift from Heaven, as a seal of Christ, that peace which the world can neither give nor take away.

I shall suffer, I shall repent, I shall do penance, I shall sacrifice myself — everything, but with peace in my heart; for I know that here is someone who loves me in spite of my infidelities; someone who, when I wander, puts me back on the right path; who, when I fall, raises me up; who, when I sink into the mud, knows how to purify me.

If we only knew Jesus, His love, and His mercy! Then fear would disappear from our souls, and on the wings of hope, we would rise above the miseries of life, and peace would establish in our hearts the kingdom of God.

## When God Is Silent

*Hope banishes fear*

Our frailty and our diffidence never cease to make objections. We are so inclined to mistrust. To be anxious seems to us so natural a thing that often we try to withdraw from the peace that God has given us. We wonder if it can be an illusion; we scrutinize to see whether we may not have reason to be disturbed. Perhaps it occurs to us to say, "How is it possible to live in peace, without uneasiness, in this sad exile, so far from our blessed Fatherland, exposed to the loss of our happiness forever? Could the Israelites live without worry when they were wandering over the desolate sands of the desert, so far from the Promised Land and so exposed to the possibility of never reaching that land overflowing with milk and honey?"

There are at least two justifiable motives for anxiety. First, will that happy day ever come in which the intense yearning of my soul for close union with God will be satisfied? Or shall I remain like Moses, contemplating the Promised Land from Mount Nebo, without ever setting foot thereon?"[60]

A second apparently legitimate reason for anxiety is this: If God loves me, if I am in His arms, from this viewpoint I should have no fear; but my frailty and my malice, which daily become more evident to me, will they not draw me away from the holy security of divine love? It is true that Jesus carries me in His arms, but do I not have the unfortunate prerogative of extricating myself? Jesus certainly loves me, but shall I also love Him? Shall I be faithful?

Do both of these causes of anxiety exist in reality? No. At first sight, they seem warranted, but our Lord placed in our soul some gifts so rich (we might even say divine) that they of themselves establish us in peace.

One of these gifts is the divine virtue of hope, a heavenly virtue, yet a forgotten virtue. How few souls, even among those consecrated to God, give

[60]Cf. Deut. 32:48-50.

this neglected virtue the importance that it deserves! Practical-minded, we are preoccupied with more human virtues, more in touch with earth: mortification, humility, obedience. Some persons look upon hope as an impractical virtue, almost useless; at least they know neither when nor how to practice it.

Nevertheless, hope is an eminently practical virtue; it is the virtue that drives far from our heart the specter of discouragement, the most frequent dangerous temptation in the spiritual life. As the inseparable companion of suffering, it confirms and strengthens peace in our soul.

Another motive of uneasiness is the preoccupation with the question of our attaining the divine union in the world and everlasting happiness in the next. In support of our fears, we hasten to quote certain scriptural passages, such as St. Peter's admonition to work out our salvation with fear and trembling.[61] *Solicitude*

[61] Phil. 2:12.

is not synonymous with *fear*, not even the fear of God. The gift of the fear of God, the beginning of wisdom,[62] is not a servile fear; it is a filial fear, the fear of the soul lest it lose its Beloved; it is a form of love. Evidently, such a fear is perfectly compatible with peace; we may say that it is one of the foundations of peace.

We can be sure that we shall attain union with God and eternal happiness, because we have God's promise, and the promises of God are realities.

Abraham received magnificent promises from God, and strange as it seems, none was to be fulfilled for four hundred years after the patriarch's time. Nevertheless, those divine promises filled his life with peace and consolation; his strong faith and hope gave him to understand that a promise of God is a reality.

Aware of man's insincerity and limitations, we do not always place credence in human promises. God's promise is reality. I have absolute certainty that what

---

[62]Ps. 111:10; Prov. 9:10.

God has promised me will be fulfilled, because Heaven and earth shall pass away but God's word shall never pass,[63] because His name, as Scripture states, is *Faithful and True*.[64] God has promised us eternal happiness, and to enable us to support the divine weight of that promise, He placed in our hearts the virtue of hope.

Divine hope is not like earthly hope. The latter is subject to disappointment, for however strong our security, it can either be realized or not realized. Who is the fortunate person who has seen all his hopes fulfilled in this world? But the theological virtue of hope is not subject to disappointment; it gives us the holy, invincible certainty that we shall obtain what God has promised.

St. Thomas,[65] whose authority is indisputable in the Church, poses a problem when treating of this

[63]Cf. Matt. 24:35.

[64]Rev. 19:11.

[65]St. Thomas Aquinas (c. 1225-1274), Dominican philosopher, theologian, and Doctor of the Church.

virtue of hope: If someone receives a revelation that he is to be condemned, what should he do? The saint does not hesitate to answer: Let him not believe it, because such a revelation would be opposed to the virtue of hope, and even if an angel from Heaven brought the message, the certainty given me by the divine virtue of hope is above all the angels of Heaven.

God has promised me eternal blessedness; that promise is as good as actual possession, for I enclose it within the confines of my impregnable hope. I do not base my hope on my liberty, so weak and fickle, nor on my limited strength, but upon the promise of God, His omnipotence, and His goodness.

Yet, someone may object that God has promised beatitude under such and such conditions. The conditions may be reduced to a single one, which was proclaimed by the angels at Bethlehem: "Peace on earth to men of good will." They did not say "to men of character," nor "to men of genius," nor "to men of good deeds," nor "to men of great virtue," but "to men of good will." When St. Thomas Aquinas's sister asked him how to obtain salvation, he answered her with one phrase: "Will it." Nothing more is necessary. The promises of God demand from us only this one condition: *Will it!*

Do we not sometimes have inward experience of the good will the angels heralded in Bethlehem? It is true that our will is weak and vacillating, but the angels promised peace not to men of energetic, constant, or strong will, but to men of *good* will.

Believe me, it takes a lot for a man to be damned — so much so, that at times I cannot explain the mystery to myself. It is not because I have no experience of man's malice and ingratitude, nor because sin seems to me a rare occurrence. No, I know that is very easy and frequent, but to be damned, it does not suffice to have sinned.[66] To be damned, it is necessary to wrestle with

[66]The meaning of this statement is easily understood. In the order of justice, one single mortal sin merits Hell and suffices for damnation. It is not so in the order of

the infinite mercy of God; to be damned, it is necessary to tear out of the heart the last vestige of good will. Therefore, hope gives us peace.

∞

The virtue of hope has another important function in this life. Hope is the inseparable companion of suffering; suffering without hope is a bitter, insupportable burden. Suffering is sometimes debilitating, oppressive, crushing. It crushed Jesus Himself, the very strength of Heaven. Did He not feel overwhelmed that night in Gethsemane? Did He not sweat blood? Was He not in agony? Did He not feel the weariness and sadness of death? Did He not exclaim, "If it be possible, let this cup pass from me"?[67]

And if suffering overwhelmed Jesus, why should it not crush our frailty? In the midst of our sufferings, we need something that will succor us in our weakness

mercy, which struggles with the sinner until the final instant of life. — ED., Spanish edition.

[67]Cf. Matt. 26:39; Luke 22:42.

and support us in our wretchedness — something that, without blunting the pain, will make us see joy and happiness in the future and thus make us capable of persevering endurance.

Jesus Christ, as St. Paul teaches, foresaw the divine joy of glorifying the Father and the joy of making us happy, and because that joy was set before Him, He endured the Cross. The Cross is so beautiful, so fruitful, so very precious! But no one can support just the Cross alone. We can endure present suffering only so far as we can foresee future joy. It was thus that Jesus endured the Cross: "Jesus . . . for the joy that was set before Him, endured the Cross, despising the shame."[68]

Therefore, hope, which holds out to us sweet joy and complete happiness, is the inseparable companion of sorrow. Suffering without hope is a sad, desolate experience; suffering with hope is a wonderful combination.

[68]Heb. 12:2.

Permit me to make a comparison that, although rather prosaic, seems suitable for clarifying my thought. Just as physicians blend certain substances so that one may counteract the effect of the other in the resultant medicine, so Jesus has made a happy combination of pain and hope. Suffering is the potent medicine of the spiritual life, hope is added to pain, and, with this combination, we can travel in peace over the dismal desert of this world with eyes and heart fixed on the promised land of eternity. Let us note that hope gives us not only the assurance of beatitude, but also the certainty of all graces for our sanctification.

Sometimes we say to God, "Lord, I promise you such and such a thing, provided You give me Your grace." Again, "If our Lord grants me His grace, I shall do this or that." It seems to me a kind of spiritual pleonasm to place this condition, "If He gives me His grace," because such a thing is not conditional but absolute. I have at hand the graces necessary for my salvation, because I have at hand the divine promise. Never will God's grace be lacking to me, because God is faithful and has promised to give me all that I need for my soul's salvation.

Of course, if I begin to desire something that God has not promised, I must include the condition, "If God wants it, if God gives me His grace."

But shall I correspond with God's grace? Shall I not be unfaithful? This is the last stand of the diffident and the discouraged. I am sure that God has promised me beatitude and that He has put into my hands the necessary graces, but shall I correspond? Shall I preserve until the end the good will that I now possess?

To destroy this last doubt of the mistrustful, I offer two invulnerable points.

The first point is that fidelity itself is a gift of God; He is able to give it to me, and Scripture assures me that He does. St. Paul declares that God gives "both the will to do it and the accomplishment of that will."[69] Since the will depends upon Him, it is not subject to the vicissitudes and the velleities of poor human frailty. Therefore, I hold fast to hope; I possess my soul in peace.

Shall I persevere in the will to be faithful?

*Lord, into Your hands I place both my will and my fidelity. I hope from You not only Your promised graces but also the will which that promise includes.*

Still another objection may need to be settled. Although my frailty is great and my amazing gift of liberty may snatch me from God's arms to cast me down the slope that leads to the abyss, I know that God loves me sufficiently either not to allow this or, if He should permit it, to come to look for me. He will descend with His love and His omnipotence along the slope that leads to destruction and He will take me in His arms, and like a good shepherd, He will place me upon His shoulders and bring

[69] Phil. 2:13 (Knox translation).

me back to the fold. No, I do not fear my weakness, for as St. Thérèse of the Child Jesus said, "I know upon what I am relying in the love and the mercy of my Savior."

If we understood these consoling truths, if we exercised and developed the virtue of hope within our own hearts, we would be established in peace, and the specter of distrust would disappear.

∞

### *Love is the loftiest path to peace*

One more path to peace remains, the loftiest, the most excellent, the most secure: charity, love.

In St. John we read, "Perfect love casts out fear."[70] He does not say that it casts out anxiety, because perfect love is not required for ridding ourselves of worry; genuine love is enough. Peace is the specific, delightful fruit of charity.

[70] 1 John 4:18.

Therefore, St. Thomas states that the beatitude of peace is the beatitude of love. "Blessed are the peacemakers, for they shall be called sons of God."[71] The peacemakers are those who love, who have concentrated all their desires into one single desire: desire for God; those who have gathered their aspirations and tenderness of soul into one closely bound bundle: the sheaf of love.

True love that has reached its maturity is a deep, solid love; it is sure of itself. It is not to be supposed that the love which St. Paul described is exclusively his own. His words reveal to us the mystery of love: "I am sure that neither death, nor life, nor angels, nor principalities, nor things present, nor things to come, nor powers, nor height, nor depth, nor anything else in all creation, will be able to separate us from the love of God in Christ Jesus our Lord."[72]

[71]Matt. 5:9.
[72]Rom. 8:38-39.

## When God Is Silent

Upon reading these words we say, "What a daring apostle!" Who else could have his assurance? Only one elevated to the third heaven,[73] the recipient of superabundant graces could be permitted such boldness. But I?" Yes. St. Paul did not speak thus because he was St. Paul, but because his heart was filled with the charity that the Holy Spirit pours into all our hearts. When this charity takes root in our soul, when it has reached maturity, we can say the same.

Love cannot possibly be taken away from us. Earthly despots and diabolical powers may take away everything else from us, but they cannot deprive us of the charity of God, which is in Christ Jesus. Only we ourselves have that unfortunate endowment. But if we truly love, shall we be so foolish, so suicidal as to tear out of our heart the charity of God?

Solid, profound, true love is sure of itself. And when, to the certainty of God's love for us, we add

[73]Cf. 2 Cor. 12:2.

the certainty of our love for Him (although a poor, miserable, inadequate love), shall we not have found at last the blessed state of interior tranquillity?

∞

*Faith, hope, and love unite you with Christ*

These are, then, the paths that lead to the summit of peace. These three ways, these three divine gifts that aid our ascent to that longed-for height, we carry in our heart: faith, hope, and love. These three virtues give us peace, because through them we touch God, because through them we embrace Jesus who, as St. Paul says, is our peace.[74]

Bound to Jesus by these divine virtues, indestructibly united with Him by hope and charity, we can pass tranquilly through the desolate sands of our exile, with eyes and heart fixed on that happy region where peace is converted into everlasting beatitude. With faith,

[74]Eph. 2:14.

hope, and charity in our soul, we can endure every suffering, saying bravely and boldly with St. Paul, "I can do all things in Him who strengthens me."[75]

Thus, consoled by God's immortal promise, bearing these divine virtues in the fragile vessel of our flesh, we shall be able to live in peace, while there resounds in our souls the echo of a hope, Bethlehem's sweet song: "Glory to God in the highest, and on earth peace to men of good will."

[75]Phil. 4:13.

*Biographical Note*

∞

## Luis M. Martinez
*(1881-1956)*

∞

"A diamond of multiple facets" is what a close, life-long friend of Archbishop Luis Martinez called this philosopher, theologian, educator, sacred orator, writer, poet, and director of souls. "But," continues his friend, "there is perhaps one aspect that has remained in shadow until now, in spite of the fact that it is the most important: it is the interior man, his spiritual life, his intimate relationship with God; in a word, it is the mystic. . . ."[76]

Luis Maria Martinez was born in Michoacán in 1881, entered the Seminary of Morelia in 1891, and

[76]J. G. Treviño, "Monseñor Martinez," *La Cruz*, no. 428:205; see also Luis M. Martinez, *True Devotion to the Holy Spirit* (Manchester, New Hampshire: Sophia Institute Press, 2000), vii.

was ordained a priest in 1904. He served the Church in numerous positions, including rector of the seminary and canon of the cathedral in Morelia, apostolic administrator for the diocese of Chilapa, Titular Bishop of Anemurio, Auxiliary Bishop of Morelia, and finally Archbishop of Mexico City.

Among his works, Archbishop Martinez encouraged the construction of a new building for the seminary, presided over a diocesan synod to respond to the needs of the time, and gave momentum to the restoration of the cathedral.

Perhaps more important than his accomplishments in his own archdiocese, though, was his contribution to the return of peace and harmony to the entire Mexican Church after the persecution by the administration of Plutarco Calles and his successors. This contribution was due in part to his action as Archbishop and to his dispositions of bonhomie and moderation, which served to win him the favor of influential leaders.

Luis M. Martinez

Although involved in the administration of his diocese and in the turbulent events of his times, Archbishop Martinez led a deeply spiritual interior life, which is manifested eloquently in his many, diverse writings. With a poetic beauty of expression, his words continue to reveal the marvelous work of God's grace in the soul, and to teach and inspire Christians to receive and increase that grace and to bear fruit in the joyful service of God.

# Sophia Institute

Sophia Institute is a nonprofit institution that seeks to nurture the spiritual, moral, and cultural life of souls and to spread the Gospel of Christ in conformity with the authentic teachings of the Roman Catholic Church.

Sophia Institute Press fulfills this mission by offering translations, reprints, and new publications that afford readers a rich source of the enduring wisdom of mankind.

Sophia Institute also operates two popular online Catholic resources: CrisisMagazine.com and CatholicExchange.com.

*Crisis Magazine* provides insightful cultural analysis that arms readers with the arguments necessary for navigating the ideological and theological minefields of the day. *Catholic Exchange* provides world news from a Catholic perspective as well as daily devotionals and articles that will help you to grow in holiness and live a life consistent with the teachings of the Church.

In 2013, Sophia Institute launched Sophia Institute for Teachers to renew and rebuild Catholic culture through service to Catholic education. With the goal of nurturing the spiritual, moral, and cultural life of souls, and an abiding respect for the role and work of teachers, we strive to provide materials and programs that are at once enlightening to the mind and ennobling to the heart; faithful and complete, as well as useful and practical.

Sophia Institute gratefully recognizes the Solidarity Association for preserving and encouraging the growth of our apostolate over the course of many years. Without their generous and timely support, this book would not be in your hands.

www.SophiaInstitute.com
www.CatholicExchange.com
www.CrisisMagazine.com
www.SophiaInstituteforTeachers.org

Sophia Institute Press® is a registered trademark of Sophia Institute.
Sophia Institute is a tax-exempt institution as defined by the
Internal Revenue Code, Section 501(c)(3). Tax I.D. 22-2548708.